Get Down to Earth!

What You Can Do to Stop Global Warming

LAURIE DAVID & CAMBRIA GORDON

ORCHARD BOOKS • NEW YORK
AN IMPRINT OF SCHOLASTIC INC.

For Micah, Arlo, and Capp, who keep me down to Earth, and for
Laurie, who opened my eyes

— C. G.

For Cazzie and Romy, so that they can finally understand what I have
been talking about, and to the staff at the Natural Resources Defense
Council — more than 300 lawyers, scientists, and policy experts who
have devoted their lives to protecting our environment

— L. D.

ISBN-13: 978-0-545-08717-9
ISBN-10: 0-545-08717-1

10 9 8 7 6 5 4 3 2 1   08 09 10 11 12
Printed in the U.S.A.   03

First edition, January 2008

Book Design by Charles Kreloff

Recycled
Supporting responsible use
of forest resources
www.fsc.org Cert no. SW-COC-002
© 1996 Forest Stewardship Council

Acknowledgments

They say that it takes a village to raise a child. Well, the authors believe that it also takes a village to write a children's book. We could not have completed this book without the help of so many. First and foremost, a thank-you to our husbands (one current and one former), Howard and Larry, who have supported our passion for the environment with both humor and love. Thank you to the experts at the Natural Resources Defense Council: Allen Hershkowitz, Andrew Wetzler, Darby Hoover, Jack Murphy, Jon Coifman, Kate Wing, Lisa Suatoni, Luke Tonachel, Nathanial Greene, and especially the ever-patient Dan Lashof, Joel Reynolds, John Steelman, and Tim Greeff for the extra time they put in to help us understand the complexities of global warming; Susan Hassol for her endless reads and thoughtful scientific assessments; Brendan DeMelle and Rachel Diamond, the best researchers any authors could ask for; Dawn Woollen and Sara Altshul for their superb attention to detail; Liana Schwarz for her unlimited knowledge, patience, and coordination of our fact-checking; Eric Wolff, Dr. Gareth Marshall, and the scientists at British Antarctic Survey; Heidi Cullen of the Weather Channel, for her grasp of wacky weather; Richard Fox of the Butterfly Conservation; Erica Levine of Community Energy, Inc.; David Zutler of Biota, for kindly responding to our inquiries; Cristina Mittermeier, Executive Director, International League of Conservation Photographers, for her willingness to lend images to this book .; and Dr. Mark Spencer, Director of the Environmental Leadership Opportunity Program, College of Natural Resources, UC Berkeley. Much appreciation goes to Judy Rothman for the impetus to do a cool kids' project on the environment; to Jennifer Jaeger at Andrea Brown Literary Agency for her undying belief in this book; Brian Lipson at Endeavor for his astute pro bono legal counsel; our gracious editor, Lisa Sandell, for her insightful comments, flag-waving enthusiasm, and vision; Amla Sanghvi, photo editor extraordinaire; Siobhán McGowan, for helping bring this book to fruition; and the incredible members of the Scholastic design team, Charles Kreloff, Kay Petronio, David Saylor, and Becky Terhune, who brought our vision to life.

Authors' Note

Since this book was written, much has happened and breaking news stories about global warming are coming fast. Here are some big developments that we learned about right as we were going to press:

The United States Supreme Court ruled that carbon dioxide and other global warming emissions are indeed pollutants under the Clean Air Act, so the Environmental Protection Agency has the authority to start cutting them. This is good news for the planet!

The Intergovernmental Panel on Climate Change (IPCC), a group made up of hundreds of scientists from around the world, concluded in its latest report that the warming of the climate system is unequivocal and very likely due to human activity. The third installment of IPCC's four-part report echoes the Stern Report, issued in England, which concluded that the costs of stabilizing the planet are significant but manageable and that the longer we wait, the more costly and dangerous it will become.

Scientists at the National Ice and Snow Center of Colorado, using satellite data and visual confirmation, found the polar ice cap to be melting much faster — 30 years faster! — than the IPCC predicted.

"Noah's Ark," a recent study by researchers at Bologna's Institute for Atmospheric Sciences and Climate Change, has concluded that many famous historical monuments are at risk from climate change. Both drought and intense rains could threaten the marble, metal, and wood in such beloved European landmarks as the Greek Parthenon, the Eiffel Tower, the Roman Colosseum, and the Tower of London.

China is expected to surpass the United States as the number one source of global warming emissions in the next year or two.

A diverse group of corporations from around the world, including General Electric, Air France, Volvo, and Citigroup, have formed the Global Round Table on Climate Change. This nonpolitical coalition is asking its governments to set targets to reduce CO_2 emissions. Similarly, corporations in the United States, including General Motors, PepsiCo, Royal Dutch Shell's U.S. subsidiary, BP America, ConocoPhillips, and Johnson & Johnson, have formed the United States Climate Action Partnership. They are also asking Congress to limit greenhouse gas emissions. This is especially notable because many of these corporations are in the oil and gas business!

Australia and Canada have voted to ban the use of regular incandescent lightbulbs by 2009 and 2012, respectively.

The city of San Francisco voted to outlaw the use of plastic checkout bags in large supermarkets by Fall 2007 and in large chain pharmacies about six months after that. In the United States and Canada, some of the biggest retailers, including Home Depot, Wal-Mart, and Ikea, and sports complexes like Boston's Fenway Park, are taking steps to promote sustainable products and reduce the carbon footprint of their stores.

Former Vice President Al Gore and the IPCC were awarded the Nobel Peace Prize in October 2007 for their work to increase awareness of global warming.

The U.S. government is working on a law that would phase out regular lightbulbs over the next seven years. The European Union, Canada, and Australia are also planning phaseouts, and China is considering it as well.

As our Earth continues to show signs of global warming, people are showing signs of action. We salute you.

So What Exactly *Is* Global Warming?

Picture this: It's late at night. You're asleep in bed, with lots of blankets covering you. Suddenly, you wake up all hot and sweaty, so you kick off the covers. Cool air hits your legs. Much better. You fall back to sleep and wake up refreshed, ready for school.

Now picture the Earth. Certain gases that have been collecting in the atmosphere for the past 100 years are creating a heavy blanket around the Earth. **Heat from the sun gets trapped under the blanket and the Earth begins to feel too hot. But the Earth can't just kick off that cover to cool down. This is global warming.**

Of all the gases in the atmosphere, carbon dioxide (CO_2) contributes the most to global warming. But CO_2 is also necessary to sustain life. CO_2 is released into the atmosphere when dead organisms decompose and volcanoes erupt. It is then absorbed by plants, which use it to grow, and by the oceans, which use it to nourish sea life, beginning with microscopic plants called algae.

Our planet is heating up.

Humans and other animals eat plants and exhale carbon dioxide when they breathe, completing the cycle. And over thousands and millions of years, much of this carbon ends up buried underground or at the bottom of the oceans.

Every living thing on planet Earth is part of the natural carbon cycle.

This is how it has always worked. But, recently, we have been asking too much of the carbon cycle. **Cars, factories, and electric power plants have been putting too much of this buried carbon into our atmosphere.**

You might be thinking, why is global warming so important now? Well, because the Earth is the only home we have. When weather patterns are altered, life as we know it will be altered, too. We'll feel the changes every season of the year, while at home or on vacation. For example, global warming is causing some summer nights to be as warm as summer days, preventing people's bodies from getting a necessary break from the heat, and this creates serious health risks. Global warming is also causing less snow to fall in the higher altitudes, so your favorite ski and snowboard spot might be closed when you get there.

Global warming is a problem that's happening now. The good news is that we still have time to solve it.

While the Earth is indeed good at absorbing carbon dioxide, it can only handle so much. If carbon dioxide were a pizza, then we are expecting the Earth to eat a whole pie rather than just one slice. In other words, we're releasing too much carbon dioxide, too fast.

A Greenhouse Gas Is Not Caused by an Orchid Grower Who Ate Too Many Beans

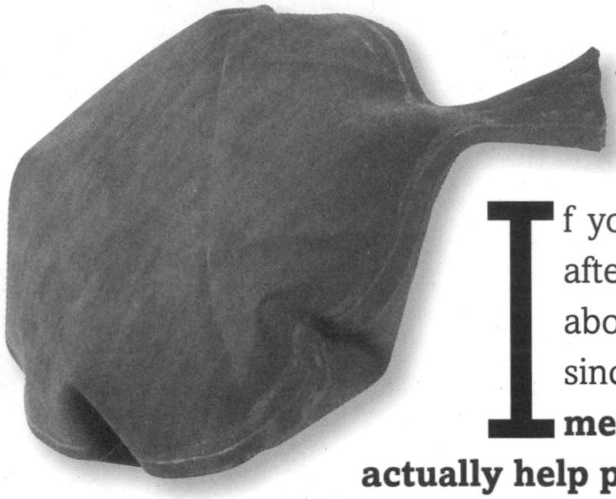

That would be gas in the greenhouse.

If you've ever eaten too many burritos, then you know what can happen afterward. But we're not talking about that kind of gas. The gases we're talking about have been floating around in our atmosphere, surrounding the Earth, since life first began. **Greenhouse gases have names like carbon dioxide, methane (which, now that you mention it, burping and farting cows actually help produce), water vapor, nitrous oxide, and more.** The reason they're called greenhouse gases is because they act just like a real glass-covered greenhouse, like the kind you could grow orchids in — or even beans. Both glass-covered greenhouses and greenhouse gases let sunlight in but prevent the warmth from escaping back out.

What Kinds of Greenhouse Gases Are in Our Air?

Carbon Dioxide 82%

Methane 9%

Nitrous Oxide 5%

Other 4%

Ever wonder where some of that methane comes from?

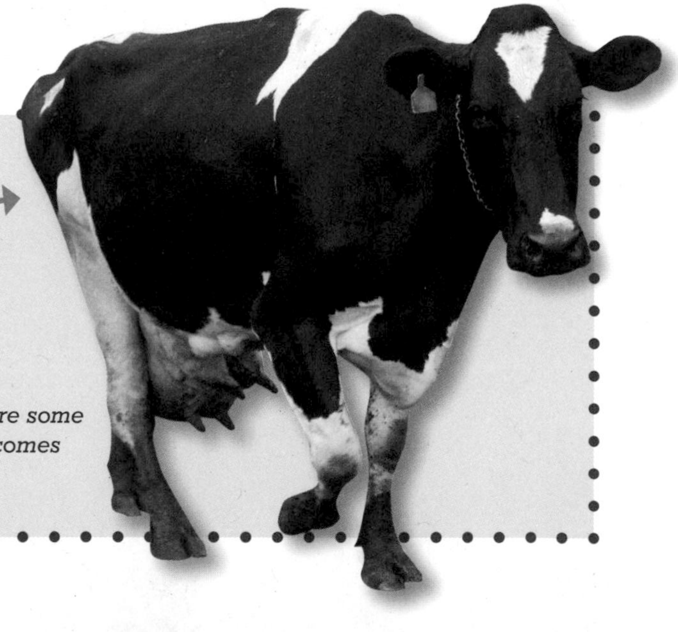

A little bit of greenhouse gas is good. It keeps our planet at a comfortable 57°F (14°C), a temperature that's averaged over the whole planet and across all the seasons. But at this point in history, we humans have released so much greenhouse gas into the atmosphere, the Earth's average temperature has actually risen one degree! Maybe you're thinking that doesn't sound so bad.

If the Earth's average temperature increases even a few degrees, gigantic changes can happen:

* Arctic sea ice and land-based ice will melt.
* Oceans will get too warm, causing fiercer hurricanes.
* Heat waves will last longer.
* Flooding will increase.
* Droughts will occur.
* Animals and plants might die because they can't adapt to the change in temperature.
* And humans can suffer, too.

Too bad the Earth can't just stop eating burritos.

Consider this:

You know that Popsicle in your freezer? At 32°F (0°C), it freezes and stays solid enough for you to bite it. But at 33°F (0.5°C), it falls off the stick.

The Greenhouse Effect

Normal Greenhouse Effect

When direct sunlight (short-wave energy) heads toward Earth, it passes right through greenhouse gases. Some of the sunlight is reflected by the clouds back into space, but most is absorbed by the Earth and is used to warm the planet's surface. The Earth then radiates some of that heat (long-wave energy) back into the atmosphere. Only then do greenhouse gases go to work, trapping long-wave energy and using it to keep the lower ten miles of our atmosphere livable.

Extreme Greenhouse Effect

With the increased amount of greenhouse gases in our atmosphere, too much long-wave energy is being trapped underneath the greenhouse blanket. The extra heat has nowhere to go but back down to Earth, warming the planet more than is healthy.

What Is Your Carbon Footprint?

Here's what it's not: when you stick your foot in a bucket of oil and step on a white rug. Here's what it is: the amount of carbon dioxide pollution that is emitted from the energy you use. Every year, each of us releases literally tons of carbon dioxide into the air. CO_2 is measured in pounds, and there are 2,000 lb (907 kg) in a ton. The average American adult emits 20 tons (18 metric tons) or 40,000 lb (18,144 kg) of CO_2 a year. And together, all human beings the world over add 100 million *tons* (91 million metric tons) of CO_2 into the atmosphere each day!

Your carbon footprint comes from normal, everyday activities like using your computer, turning on the light in your bedroom, taking a bath (heating water uses energy!), and riding in a bus or car to school. So let's take a moment and do some simple math to calculate your carbon footprint. Don't worry, you won't get graded on it. **But we hope you'll start to make the connection between how you live and your personal daily contribution to global warming.**

There is a number that represents how much CO_2 the atmosphere can hold before the harmful effects of global warming become unstoppable. It's an amount that scientists call the carbon budget. Every pound of carbon dioxide we put into the atmosphere is bringing us closer to reaching the limits of our budget.

Here are some average statistics for the average kid on an average day:

❊ **Using a screen saver on the computer (based on an LCD monitor) emits 2.5 lb (1.1 kg) of carbon dioxide.**

❊ **Turning on the lights (based on three 60-watt bulbs in a ceiling fixture kept on for six hours a day) will generate 1.5 lb (680 g) of carbon dioxide.**

❊ **Taking a bath uses up to 3.5 lb (1.6 kg) of carbon dioxide. (Hint: Taking a two-minute shower is better!)**

❊ **Riding in a car to school uses 5 lb (2.3 kg) of CO_2 (based on driving to school 2.5 miles (4 km) each way in a car that gets 20 miles (32 km) per gallon).**

Total = 12.5 lb (5.7 kg) of carbon dioxide per day

Now, if you take your daily number and multiply that by the number of kids between the ages of eight and 16 in the whole world, which is about 1.2 billion (that number looks like this: 1,200,000,000), that's more than 15.24 *billion* lb (6.9 billion kg) of

carbon dioxide per day! The Earth can handle only so much carbon.

Think about your bedroom closet. You fill it with clothes, shoes, board games, sports equipment, books, old toys, and suitcases. You can keep putting stuff in there, but there's a point at which the closet will be full. After that, put one more thing in there, even if it's something as small as a tennis ball, and everything will come toppling down on your head.

Every pound of CO_2 takes up space in the atmosphere. That's why it's so important to conserve energy. We don't want to use up our carbon budget. Luckily, there are lots of simple ways we can reduce our carbon footprints right away.

The Day After Tomorrow

Because CO_2 stays in the atmosphere for decades or more, almost half of the CO_2 you put in the atmosphere today will still be there when your grandchildren are born. This is why the problem of global warming is so urgent. Everything we do today means that we, and our families, are going to be living with the consequences tomorrow. We need to make a change and do things better.

Clean Up Your Room!

If you're like most kids, your room probably could use a little cleaning up. And if your mom's like most moms, she's probably been nagging you about it. She's right, by the way. You made the mess. You should clean it up. Well, the planet is kind of like one big messy bedroom. And guess what? The United States is making the biggest mess of all. We produce 25 percent of the world's carbon dioxide, making us the biggest polluter on the planet. So we need to play the largest part in helping to clean it up.

Mayors in cities all across America have signed an agreement to lower CO_2 emissions in their towns. The idea began in Seattle with Mayor Greg Nickels. It's called the U.S. Mayors Climate Protection Agreement, and its goal is to cut greenhouse gas emissions to levels below what they were in 1990 by 2012.

Here's what some cities have already done: Portland, Oregon, built 730 miles (1,175 km) of bike paths; Austin, Texas, gave tax breaks to homes and businesses for building green structures; Salt Lake City, Utah, converted 1,630 traffic signals to energy-efficient lightbulbs.

To find out if your mayor has already signed the agreement, check the Web site www.coolcities.us. If your city isn't listed there, then make a copy of the letter on page 13, stick it in an envelope, and send it to your mayor. If your city *is* there, do a victory dance, then find another city you've always liked and send the letter to its mayor. **The more mayors, the less CO_2!**

California, Here We Come!

Under the leadership of Governor Arnold Schwarzenegger, the state of California passed a landmark bill that made it the first state to limit global warming pollution. California has pledged to reduce carbon dioxide emissions to 1990 levels by the year 2020, and it also pledges to bring down levels to 80 percent below 1990 levels by the year 2050. We hope that other states across the nation will follow this example.

Cyclists take advantage of the new bike paths in Portland, Oregon.

To find out the name and address of a mayor, go to www.usmayors.org.

Dear Mayor _____,

Global warming is real and it's here to stay — unless we do something to stop it. There's an amazing agreement that more than 400 of your fellow mayors have signed. It's called the U.S. Mayors Climate Protection Agreement. It's a 12-step program that sets reasonable goals for your city to reduce carbon dioxide emissions to below what the levels were in 1990. Please join these other mayors in being leaders in the fight to stop global warming.

The kids of the world are depending on you.

Sincerely,

_____, Age_____

Or go paperless . . .

Check www.scholastic.com/downtoearthguide to download and e-mail this letter to your mayor!

How Many Concerned Kids Does It Take to Screw in a Lightbulb?

One. As long as it's a compact fluorescent bulb.

We think Thomas Edison would be thrilled to know that someone one-upped him by inventing a better lightbulb. It's not that his lightbulb wasn't incredible, it's just that all lightbulbs use electricity, which burns fossil fuels, which release greenhouse gases into the atmosphere and cause global warming. So why not try a bulb that uses *less* electricity and therefore releases *less* carbon dioxide?

A compact fluorescent lightbulb is 75% more energy-efficient than a regular lightbulb.

If you put a regular 60-watt incandescent bulb into a light you keep on most of the day, you might get 800 lumens for two months before it burns out. Lumens is a fancy-schmancy word for the total amount of light that a bulb is capable of generating.

With a 15-watt compact fluorescent bulb, you get 800 lumens for 20 months — ten times longer!

Compact fluorescent bulbs do the same amount of work as incandescents, yet use less energy, emit less CO_2, and last longer. It's like getting an upgrade on your iTunes software. Compact fluorescents are *new and improved* lightbulbs! If we sound like a commercial, we can't help it. This is an exciting and easy way to help stop global warming.

The reason compact fluorescent bulbs use less energy is they produce much less heat — which for a lightbulb is just wasted energy, because we only need the light. Touch a lit compact fluorescent bulb and it will feel cool.

Regular lightbulbs use four times more energy than compact fluorescent bulbs. Four times more is the equivalent of having four PlayStations instead of one. **What a waste.** You might even feel embarrassed by having so much. Similarly, we don't need all that wattage; we're using more than we need to do the job. The wasted electricity just burns more fossil fuels.

Though some compact fluorescent bulbs cost more than incandescent bulbs, you can end up saving at least 30 dollars on your family's electric bill over the life of the bulb.

Change a lightbulb today. All it takes is one person. And maybe a ladder.

A Bright Idea . . .

If every kid in America swapped one regular bulb for a compact fluorescent, we could prevent more than 30 *billion* pounds (13.6 billion kg) of greenhouse gas emissions and save enough energy to light more than 15 million homes for an entire year. It would be like taking 14 million cars off the road.

Gulp!

That's *plug* spelled backward, for all you word game experts. The reason why this page isn't called "plug" is because we want you to think about plugs differently and *un*plug your chargers. Believe it or not, leaving a charger plugged into the wall even after you remove your cell phone, iPod, GAME BOY, radio-controlled toy car, or MP3 player still drains energy. Plugged-in chargers use what's called phantom power, or standby power. In other words, it's power that you don't need and that is wasted. Just like Thomas Edison's hot lightbulb. Touch the plugged-in charger and it's warm.

Is Your Refrigerator *Running*?

The typical home contributes two times more global warming pollution than the average car. Because it is always running, the refrigerator is the single biggest energy-eating appliance in your house. To reduce your carbon footprint at home, urge your parents to buy appliances with a blue- or black-and-white ENERGY STAR sticker.

Saving or conserving what we don't need to use is one of the many solutions to global warming.

Actually, quite a large amount of home electricity is used up by phantom power. **Up to 10 percent of what your parents get billed for is stuff you turn off but don't unplug.** This includes not only chargers but televisions, computers, DVD players, even blow-dryers and electric toothbrushes.

The solution is simple. **Unplug those chargers from the wall. For all your appliances that you keep in one spot, like the computer and printer, or the TV, DVD player, and satellite or cable box, get a surge protector.** These are the long, funny-looking things with eight outlets for plugs that work like a normal power strip, only they're more efficient because they have an off switch that completely cuts off power from plugged-in appliances. **At the end of the day, turn off the surge protector.** It's just one switch and it can do a whole lot of good. Or *doog*.

Give It a Rest

Using the screen saver feature on your computer actually uses more energy than letting your computer go into sleep mode. Check the control panel or settings on your computer to make your computer automatically go into sleep mode after a few minutes. That screen saver with the 3-D shapes swirling around might be totally cool, but it's better to cool off planet Earth.

Paper or Plastic? Neither!

Next time you go to the grocery store with your parents or friends and the cashier asks you, "Paper or plastic?" say, "Neither!" Canvas bags are the way to go.

Frankly, it's hard to say which is worse, paper or plastic. Americans use 10 billion paper bags a year. Most brown bags are made of kraft paper, which is stronger than other paper. The only way to get paper that tough is to blend in virgin pulp — that is, pulp made from actual trees, not from recovered paper. Some of those trees come from old-growth forests that are more than 100 years old. **Think how much CO_2 is being released when those trees are cut down and how much they won't be able to capture in the future.** Not to mention the CO_2 pollution that goes into the air when the paper and pulp mills make all that paper.

Fact: To make 14 plastic bags, you'd need the same amount of petroleum that it would take to drive a car one mile (1.6 km).

Plastic bags are made from petroleum (that's oil, guys). Petroleum, taken out of the ground, is put through several chemical reactions until, finally, a puttylike material called a polymer is created. The polymer is the basis for all plastic. Although oil isn't being burned, it's certainly being wasted on the 100 billion bags that are thrown out each year.

Here is a perfect example of where we can conserve. **Oil is a nonrenewable resource. One day it will simply run out.** If everyone used reusable canvas bags, think of all the petroleum that would be saved. Of course, the real problem with plastic bags and other plastic products like water bottles comes from the manufacturing end. The plastic industry is responsible for a significant amount of carbon dioxide emissions.

Tote a canvas bag to the mall. For every store where you buy something, you save a plastic bag.

In terms of carrying your stuff around, canvas bags are a fantastic solution. No need to double-bag your heavy groceries with virgin fiber when you've got strong canvas supporting them. Ask your parents to keep a few in the car so you'll never have to choose between paper or plastic again.

An Emerald Green Solution

In Ireland, customers are charged money for paper or plastic bags. Almost no one takes them now!

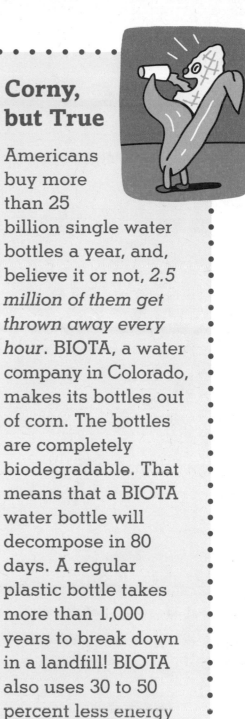

Corny, but True

Americans buy more than 25 billion single water bottles a year, and, believe it or not, *2.5 million of them get thrown away every hour.* BIOTA, a water company in Colorado, makes its bottles out of corn. The bottles are completely biodegradable. That means that a BIOTA water bottle will decompose in 80 days. A regular plastic bottle takes more than 1,000 years to break down in a landfill! BIOTA also uses 30 to 50 percent less energy to make their bottles.

The Carbon (Re)Cycle

Hopefully, you already recycle. Maybe you separate your newspapers, bottles, and cans at home. Maybe you hand down your clothes to someone younger than you when you grow out of them. That's recycling, too. But in terms of global warming, paper recycling can make a difference. And just like making plastic bags, making paper uses a lot of energy. So the more we recycle paper or even do without it, the more energy we can save.

The more trees we cut down to make paper, the more CO_2 is released into the atmosphere and the fewer trees are left standing to absorb all the new CO_2 we've yet to produce.

Redwood trees of Muir Woods in northern California.

Here are some thoughts on reusing paper:

❀ That decaf mocha you or your parents like to take out from your favorite coffee place is probably served in a paper cup that used up a lot of energy to get from the tree into your hand. **Bringing in your own ceramic or travel mug with a lid saves the Earth 77.42 pounds (35.1 kg) of CO_2 over the entire life of the mug.**

❀ Your toilet paper, tissues, and paper towels are more than likely made from pulp that came from old-growth forests. Last year, one major paper products company used more than 2.7 million tons (2.5 million metric tons) of virgin timber to make its tissues, toilet paper, and paper towels, and destroyed hundreds of acres of Canada's ancient boreal forest in the process. Compare this with a company like Seventh Generation, which uses recycled fiber in nearly all of its pulp products. When you're at the store with your parents, check out the packages. **You want to buy paper goods that say they are made from 30 percent or more post-consumer waste.** (*Post-consumer waste* simply means stuff that has already been used.) Forty percent of the fiber in the world's toilet paper and tissues comes from trees never before touched by human hands. Should we be using ancient forests to wipe our noses?

❀ Your birthday cards are made from trees. **Fifteen trees are cut down and used to make one ton (907 kg) of the high-end glossy paper used in cards, magazines, and catalogs.** Another commonly used item, wrapping paper, is almost never made from recyclable material. Until there is recycled wrapping paper, you can use newspaper, discarded drawings and artwork, old magazines, even fabric remnants to wrap presents.

There are so many ways to recycle paper; these are just a few. Maybe you can come up with your own ideas and pass them on to someone else. That's what we call recycling!

Real Winners

Mountain Home High School, in Mountain Home, Arkansas, collected more than 6 million tons (5.4 million metric tons) of paper for recycling and received the 2006 School Recycling Award from the American Forest & Paper Association.

Think about what you use, how you use it, and where it goes when you're done.

Reading, Writing, and Saving Energy

We'd like to suggest that, in addition to all the things you're thinking about every day at school, like math tests and getting a good spot in line at the handball court, you think about another subject: saving energy.

Here are a few suggestions:

❀ **Start a no-idle rule in your school's car-pool lane.** Cars that sit for more than 30 seconds with their engines running use up more gasoline and emit more global warming pollution than if the motor is turned off and on again.

❀ **Suggest changing the paper in your school.** Talk to the folks in the main office and see if they use recycled paper. If they do, the packaging will say so. It should be made from at least 30 percent post-consumer waste. If not, ask them to make the change to help save trees that soak up carbon dioxide. If that doesn't work, circulate a school petition. Make sure your school makes photocopies on both sides of the paper!

❊ **Carpool with a friend.** Traveling together means there is one less car on the road, so you're cutting the car travel portion of your carbon footprint in half.

❊ **Reduce your school's carbon footprint by finding out the age of the school's water heater.** If it's older than five years, it's inefficient, which means too much CO_2 is being released when heating the water. Maybe there's enough money in the facilities budget to replace it.

❊ **Ask your principal about getting solar panels on the roof.** Across the country, elementary, middle, and high schools, as well as colleges, have installed solar panels to supplement or generate their own electricity. They are saving money and stopping global warming at the same time.

❊ **Start a no-waste policy in the cafeteria.** All food brought in must be in reusable containers. And all trash must go home with you. This helps kids and parents see how much is wasted at lunchtime. Five juice boxes in a week should give you a good idea. You should leave nothing but a warm bench where you sat for lunch.

❊ **Choose global warming as a topic for your next science, English, or social studies report.**

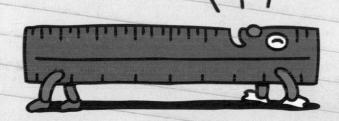

Campus Crusaders

Colleges are starting to do their part to stop global warming, too. The students of the University of Washington in Seattle agreed to raise their own fees so the school can start buying renewable electricity. At Texas A&M, they are using the cooking oil from the cafeteria to fuel the university's delivery trucks. The University of Miami offers a 50 percent parking discount for hybrid cars. And Cambridge University in England had a "Switch Off Day," reducing their electricity usage by around 5 percent just by taking simple steps like switching off unwanted lights and turning off computer monitors and printers. Imagine how much energy could be saved by doing this all year.

Once you've mastered this subject, you can even teach others about how to save energy!

✿ **Conduct a recycling drive.** Bring what you collect to a local recycling center, where they might even pay you per pound!

✿ **Put your money where your mouth is.** Take the money that your school makes on its next fund-raiser (whether it's selling chocolates or having a walkathon) and buy the school new compact fluorescent lightbulbs to replace their inefficient ones.

✿ **Host an assembly on global warming.** Invite a speaker, pick up the DVDs *Too Hot Not to Handle* from HBO and *An Inconvenient Truth* (both produced by one of the authors of this book!), and have a discussion about global warming.

✿ **Make global warming a community service project for your communion, confirmation, bar/bat mitzvah, or quinceañera.** You can donate a portion of your gift money or volunteer at an environmental organization.

Become Famous

(All You Need Is Energy)

Thirty fifth-grade students at Cherringon Elementary in Westerville, Ohio, created an energy club called the Wacky Watts. At Meece Middle School in Somerset, Kentucky, students took a field trip to a power plant, which inspired them to adopt a dock and clean up the water near their school. Other schools have received grant money to set up solar panels on campus. One group of students has even driven a hydrogen fuel cell car to other schools for demonstrations.

Why are all these kids famous? Because they were recognized at the National Youth Awards for Energy Achievement in Washington, D.C., and had their pictures taken with their representative in the U.S. Congress.

You and your school can become famous, too! All you have to do is submit your energy project to the National Energy Education Development — NEED, for short. **For more information about the NEED Awards program, please call (703) 257-1117 or go to www.need.org.**

Remember, knowledge is power: alternative energy power. Becoming famous is just a bonus.

The roof of Twenhofel Middle School in Independence, Kentucky, is lined with solar panels, which generate electricity.

Hybrid (hī-brəd)

_n._ Something of Mixed Origin or Composition

If you cross a plum and an apricot, you get a pluot. Really. If you cross a soccer ball with a basketball, you get a socket. Not really. But if you cross a gasoline engine with a battery-powered motor, you _do_ get a hybrid car.

A hybrid is high-tech, gets great gas mileage, earns your parents a tax break, and, best of all, it cuts greenhouse gas pollution. You fill up the tank at a regular gas station, only less often, and you don't have to plug it in. A hybrid car knows just when to use battery power and when to use engine power. It's also wonderfully peaceful at stop signs and red lights because the engine turns off when the car isn't moving.

How smart is that?

When this book went to press, there were hybrids on the road made by Honda, Lexus, Toyota, Ford, Mercury, Saturn, and Chevrolet. In 2008, drivers will be able to choose among 25 hybrid models. Just think how many there will be when you learn to drive! Next time you're on a road trip, play "count the hybrids." Your parents will start to notice them, too, and when they're ready for a new car, maybe they'll get their own hybrid.

We Love New York!

New York City has the largest fleet of hybrid buses in America. Now the city is converting its taxicabs into hybrids, too. Besides making passengers queasy from all that crazy driving, old NYC taxicabs get only 14 miles (22.5 km) to the gallon. A hybrid taxi can get 36 miles (58 km) to the gallon with one-third the greenhouse gas emissions!

The Alternatives Rock

The good news is that there are already great alternative fuels that provide clean substitutes for oil.

Ethanol

Ethanol is an alcohol-based fuel made from turning starch crops (like corn, barley, and wheat) into simple sugars. When combined with regular gasoline, it's called E85, which means 85 percent ethanol and 15 percent gasoline. Already widely used in Sweden and Brazil, ethanol can help reduce your car's greenhouse gas emissions, and nearly all 50 U.S. states have pump stations that now offer this type of alternative fuel.

Flex-fuel vehicles are cars that run on both gas and ethanol. It costs very little to turn a regular car into a flex-fuel vehicle, and there are about five million of them on the road in the United States today. Made by all the major carmakers, flex-fuel vehicles definitely use less gas, but the best of both worlds is the hybrid flex-fuel car. Ford, for example, is making one now.

Filling up a greaso car, which runs solely on vegetable oil.

Fact: One less barrel of imported oil is needed for every 28.3 gallons (107 l) of ethanol used.

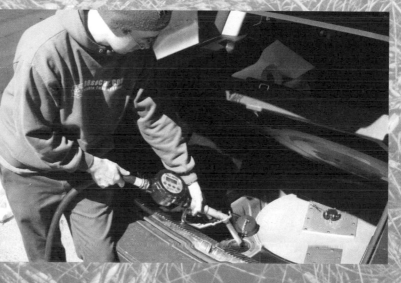

27

Biodiesel

Biodiesel, another alternative fuel, is made from a mixture of vegetable oil and alcohol, and can power any diesel engine. Some people have gone a step further and converted their modern diesels to run only on vegetable oil. The only side effect we've heard about is an unusual craving for French fries.

Speedy Clean

The Indy 500 is now using 100 percent fuel-grade ethanol to power its cars. An engine running on ethanol performs better than one that runs on regular gasoline, and track records have already been broken. And because this type of ethanol packs more energy per gallon than traditional race car fuel, these race cars can go faster and farther.

Since biodiesel is made from crops grown by farmers in the United States, it can help us become less dependent on fuels imported from other countries.

We've Got the Power

We've spent a lot of time talking about why burning fossil fuels is so bad. Now it's time to hear about why the future of fuel is good. There are other ways we can get our electricity, drive our cars, and manufacture our products. It's called renewable energy, meaning energy that won't run out and that pollutes less. Much less. It can also renew the wallet, so to speak, because governments and corporations around the world that have chosen renewable energy have seen their economies grow by creating new jobs and saving on energy costs. Here are some examples.

All together, wind machines in the United States can produce enough electricity to power a city the size of Chicago.

Wind Power

From the time of the ancient Phoenicians, the world's first sailors, people have known how to use the wind for power. The Dutch were the first to harness wind power on land, using windmills to pump water from the Rhine River in the 1600s. Today, a typical wind turbine — or a really big windmill — can generate enough power to run electricity in more than 1,000 homes.

A Stinky Solution

When animals eat hay and grain, the carbohydrate energy stored in the plant food can be found in their poop. One farm in Wisconsin actually uses cow dung to make electricity. As the cow waste breaks down, it releases methane gas. A manure digester machine speeds up this process and captures the methane. The gas is then used to fuel a small power plant. This process also prevents the methane from escaping into the atmosphere, where it would become a heat-trapping greenhouse gas!

Some people are helping to stop global warming by using the green power option on their electric bill. By paying a small amount (about $3 if your bill is $50 a month) to run wind turbines, the electric company doesn't need to burn as much coal. If more homes and businesses use the green power option, the price of wind power will go down even more!

Solar Power

Though the sun is about 93 million miles (150 million km) away from Earth, it can power anything from pool heaters to cars as long as it is harnessed properly. Solar panels (also called photovoltaic cells), solar hot water systems, and solar-thermal (thermal = heat) power stations are three ways to use the sun's energy. They work by collecting the sun's heat and transferring that energy through pipes to your home or directly to the grid that supplies power to a whole city. Some solar power systems also store energy so you have reserve power even when the sun goes down.

The 2006 Dell-Winston School Solar Car Challenge, with cars powered by nothing but the sun.

Geothermal Power

The word *geothermal* literally means "Earth heat." If you traveled 10,000 feet (3,048 m) belowground, the temperature of the rock would be hot enough to boil water. (If water deep down in the Earth gets heated by this rock and comes up through a crack in the Earth's surface, this phenomenon is called a hot spring or a geyser.) In Iceland, many buildings and swimming pools are heated with geothermal hot water. **Even power plants can run on geothermal power.** Holes are drilled into the ground and pipes are lowered into the steam or hot water, like an eyedropper is inserted into eyedrops. The hot water feeds into a turbine with spinning blades. The shaft from the turbine is connected to a generator to make electricity. If you've ever seen a geothermal power plant, that isn't smoke coming out of it, but steam being released in the cooling process. **Geothermal energy isn't used much right now, but research is under way to learn how to get heat from the deep, dry rocks inside the Earth's crust and, possibly, even deeper, from the Earth's magma.**

Old Faithful Geyser, in Yellowstone National Park.

31

Hydropower

If you've ever been tossed and turned about by an ocean wave, then you understand the power of water. Hydropower uses moving water, either from rivers or dams, to create energy. A hydroelectric dam works by holding back water behind a wall. The water is released through a pipe and pushed against blades in a turbine, causing them to turn. The turbine then spins a generator and makes electricity, which travels over long distances to your home, school, and favorite corner store.

The Grand Coulee Dam is located on the Columbia River in Washington State.

Fact: 20% of the world's electricity comes from waterpower.

Biomass Power

Believe it or not, dead trees, yard clippings, wood chips, straw, underbrush, switch grass, and composting material can produce electricity, heat, and fuel. Before this stuff was trash, it was alive, which means it was part of the carbon cycle. And that means it stored energy in the form of carbon. When the plants were alive, the photosynthesis process took the sun's energy and converted it to carbohydrates. That energy is recaptured when biomass is burned in huge boilers. The heat released from this process is used to turn water into steam, which turns a steam turbine to create electricity. Recent discoveries have even found a way to convert leaves and plant stalks into the alternative fuel ethanol.

If we used just one-eighth of what the world produces in biomass each year, it would provide all the energy needs of every single person on the planet.

There is no single solution. In fact, we need *every* solution. The future holds even more solutions, and you'll be a part of that.

33

What Do You Want to Be When You Grow Up?

A Sustainable Career

If something is sustainable, it will last and never be depleted. Your love for your pet is sustainable, even though your cat might pee on your bedspread or your dog might chew your favorite flip-flops. Bamboo, a quick-growing grass that is planted just for the purpose of constructing furniture and floors, is sustainable. Wind and solar power are sustainable.

It's never too early to dream about what you want to be when you grow up. Here are a few careers that you might want to think about:

Forest Resource Officer

Promotes respect for the web of life in a forest ecosystem. Takes action to protect the biodiversity of forests and selects species for reforestation. Can work in national parks, universities, or recycled-paper mills.

Glacial Geologist

Focuses on the Earth's past and present as it relates to the physical properties and movement of glaciers and ice sheets. Discovers how glaciers were formed and what has happened to them since their formation. Can work as a university professor or in an engineering firm.

Hydrologist

Studies the physical properties of underground and surface water. Examines rain — its rate of infiltration into the soil, its movement through the Earth, and its return to the ocean and atmosphere. Studies flood control and groundwater contamination issues. Can work as an environmental consultant in an architectural firm or for the Department of Defense.

Environmental Communicator

Gathers support to protect threatened ecosystems. Informs people about crucial environmental issues through newspaper or magazine stories, Web sites, videos, films, and photographs that show sustainable living and showcase nature. Can work for the government, in radio or television, or at museums.

Agricultural Technologist

Helps farmers with planning, cultivating, harvesting, and storing crops. Demonstrates environmentally sustainable farming techniques and suggests what crops to grow in particular soils and growing conditions. Can work in a small village or a big city.

Wind Development Associate

Helps with the construction of wind farms. Analyzes wind, sites, and environmental data. Can work at either a wind farm or a corporate office.

A career in the environmental field is sustainable because, in the future, we will need more and more experts who understand global warming.

Biofuels Engineer

Produces renewable fuels such as biodiesel, biomass, ethanol, and biogas. Can work at a biofuel plant and travel to farms where seed crops are grown.

Solar Sales Representative

Designs solar power systems for homes or businesses and convinces people to switch to solar power. Can work for a solar energy firm but can also do some work from home.

Atmospheric Scientist, or Meteorologist

Predicts the weather. Identifies climate trends by studying past and present weather. Studies air pressure, temperature, humidity, and wind speed. Can work for the government at weather stations or in broadcasting.

There are so many wonderful careers in the environmental field that it would have taken 20 more pages to list them all. We didn't think we could "sustain" your interest for that long.

Live for Today, but Protect the Future

Former Norwegian prime minister Gro Harlem Brundtland is credited with introducing the groundbreaking concept of "sustainable development" onto the world stage. The idea is that everyone — businesspeople, politicians, farmers, doctors, lawyers, environmentalists, parents, and schoolchildren, too — is responsible for creating a healthy and happy world today that will ensure the ability of future generations to meet their own needs for a healthy and happy tomorrow.

What Else You Can Do

Let Your Fingers Do the Marching

In August 1963, when Martin Luther King, Jr., led the March on Washington, 250,000 people marched along with him in support of civil rights for blacks and minorities. It was the largest demonstration ever held in the U.S. capital. In April 1970, millions turned up in cities all over the United States for the first celebration of Earth Day. In fact, the Earth Day events led to the passage of two landmark laws, the Clean Air Act and the Endangered Species Act, as well as the formation of the Environmental Protection Agency (EPA).

The thing about marches is that they generally last only one day. But now there's a way to march to stop global warming every day. It's called a virtual march and it's as easy to do as browsing and clicking. **The idea is to get as many people as possible to use the Internet instead of the pavement to register their concern for the environment. The message you'll be telling our leaders is that we want solutions to global warming. Now.**

Go to www.stopglobalwarming.org. When you see some of the other folks who are marching virtually, you'll know what good company you're in.

C. C. + S.

It's not someone's initials on the bathroom wall. It stands for Carbon Capture and Storage, and the name says it all. This is a way to prevent carbon dioxide emissions from getting into our atmosphere in the first place. Here are just two areas in which energy companies are currently doing research:

1. Capturing CO_2 from the smokestacks of power plants and feeding it to a hothouse of hungry algae.

2. Burying CO_2 deep in the ground by pumping it from the power plant directly into old oil and natural gas fields.

Carbon Capture and Storage is an exciting solution. And it lasts a lot longer than a school crush.

Go Carbon Neutral

The band Coldplay went a step further than marching. They made their carbon footprint disappear. Making an album uses up a lot of energy, from running the recording studio to producing all of those CD jewel boxes to driving the trucks and planes that have to get them to the stores. After they cut their CD *A Rush of Blood to the Head*, Coldplay bought 10,000 mango trees for villagers in Karnataka, India. The idea is that the trees will provide a carbon sink for all the CO_2 the band emitted in making and selling its CD. Of course, we can't plant enough trees to absorb all the CO_2 released from the amount of fossil fuels we are burning now, but it's one of the many things we can do.

There are many companies that can help a rock band — or a family — go carbon neutral. Here are two of them: www.carbonfund.org and www.nativeenergy.com.

Come Up with the Next Great Idea

You never know who or where a solution will come from. A ski resort in Andermatt, Switzerland, figured that since their glacier was melting, they'd protect it from heat, solar energy, and rain. They covered the whole glacier, an area more than 32,300 square feet (3,000 m²) wide, with insulating foam — kind of like putting the glacier in a giant thermos. It cost a bundle, but the insulation can be reused after every ski season.

A company called Simple Shoes recycles car tires and plastic milk jugs to make shoes for both kids and adults, saving the energy it would take if they made shoes from new rubber and plastic. Their shoes also contain materials from other renewable sources like cork trees and jute bushes, which don't require the cutting of old-growth trees to get at the stuff inside. The flip-flops even make tire-tread marks when you walk on the beach!

Kenny Luna, an eighth-grade teacher in New York, challenged everyone in his school and the surrounding community to change one lightbulb to a compact fluorescent bulb and even got Home Depot to donate the bulbs.

Anne Lasker, an elementary school parent in Los Angeles, started a Trashion Show, where kids make their outfits out of recycled material.

And an eighth-grade boy in California made a CD of original songs that he wrote and recorded at home on his computer. He then sold the CDs at school and donated the money to a stop global warming cause.

Become a Global Warming Activist

We hope you will become a global warming activist. If you can change the way you think, you can help others change the way they think. If you can make one small change in your actions, like unplugging a charger from the wall, then you'll set an example for others to do it, too. **We need big, bold ideas for this global problem.** So let's all get down to Earth and start thinking. No idea is too outrageous. No solution is too far from possibility. Will you be the one to come up with a new solution?

The Earth is depending on you!

Suggestions for Further Reading

Braasch, Gary. *Earth under Fire: How Global Warming Is Changing the World*. Berkeley, Ca.: University of California Press, 2007.

David, Laurie, and Cambria Gordon. *The Down-to-Earth Guide to Global Warming*. New York: Orchard Books, 2007.

Gore, Al. *An Inconvenient Truth: The Crisis of Global Warming*. New York: Viking Children's Books, 2007.

Langley, Andrew. *Hurricanes, Tsunamis and Other Natural Disasters*. Boston: Kingfisher, 2006.

Revkin, Andrew. *The North Pole Was Here: Puzzles & Perils at the Top of the World*. Boston: Kingfisher, 2006.

Sussman, Art, Ph.D. *Dr. Art's Guide to Planet Earth*. White River Junction, Vt.: Chelsea Green, 2000.

———. *Dr. Art's Guide to Science*. Hoboken, N.J.: Jossey Bass, 2006.

Taylor, Barbara. *How to Save the Planet*. New York: Franklin Watts, 2000.

Vogel, Carole Garbuny. *Human Impact (The Restless Sea)*. New York: Franklin Watts, 2003.

Cool Web Sites to Check Out

adventureecology.com
Here's the interactive game that lets you travel the world as an eco-adventurer to find global warming hot spots.

planetfriendly.com
This Web site certifies products, places, and processes that help the planet instead of harming it. One of the things you'll discover is plates, cups, straws, and other food containers made from corn. Look for them at the food court in your mall and at supermarket salad bars.

stopglobalwarming.org

You can sign up here for the virtual march and also order the coolest accessories around: leather bracelets that say STOP GLOBAL WARMING and flip-flops that have the Stop Global Warming logo on the straps.

stopglobalwarming.msn.com
On this MSN Web site, you can get up-to-the-minute global warming news and energy saving tips, and watch videos or read interviews of your favorite athletes, musicians, and actors talking about global warming. Windows Live Spaces will also help you create your own blog about global warming.

nrdc.org
This is the official Web site for the Natural Resources Defense Council, one of the world's best watchdogs for our environment. Click on "Kids Make Waves" to learn all about the many ways you can help.

scholastic.com/ downtoearthguide
This Web site will provide even more down-to-Earth facts and background information on this book, including downloadables, e-cards, and more.

Source Notes

Page 2 *The third installment of IPCC's four-part report* . . . : IPCC, 2007: Climate Change 2007: The Physical Science Basis. Contribution of Working Group I to the Fourth Assessment Report of the Intergovernmental Panel on Climate Change [Solomon, S., D. Qin, M. Manning, Z. Chen, M. Marquis, K. B. Avery, M. Tignor and H. L. Miller (eds.)]. Cambridge University Press, Cambridge, United Kingdom and New York, NY, USA.

Page 2 *the Stern Report, issued in England* . . . : Stern, N., et al. *The Economics of Climate Change: The Stern Review.* HM Treasury: London, 2006. Accessed online May 9, 2007, at http://www.hm-treasury.gov.uk/independent_reviews/stern_review_economics_climate_change/sternreview_index.cfm.

Page 2 *Scientists at the National* . . . : Stroeve, J., et al. "Arctic sea ice decline: Faster than forecast." *Geophysical Research Letters,* Vol. 34, L09501, doi:10.1029/2007GL029703 (2007).

Page 2 *"Noah's Ark"* . . . : Poggioli, Sylvia. "Climate Change Threatens European Landmarks." *NPR Morning Edition* 17 August 2007.

Page 2 *China is expected* . . . : Bradsher, Keith. "China to Pass U.S. in 2009 in Emissions." *The New York Times* 7 November 2006; Collier, Robert. "A Warming World: China about to pass U.S. as world's top generator of greenhouse gases." *San Francisco Chronicle* 5 March 2007.

Page 3 *Australia and Canada* . . . : "Canada to ban incandescent lightbulbs by 2012." *Reuters* 25 April 2007.

Page 3 *The city of San Francisco* . . . : Goodyear, Charlie. "S.F. First City to Ban Plastic Shopping Bags." *San Francisco Chronicle* 28 March 2007.

Page 3 *including Home Depot* . . . : *Sierra Magazine* May/June 2007, p. 33.

Page 3 *like Boston's Fenway Park* . . . : Van Voorhis, Scott. "Wally Would Be Proud as Fenway Park Goes Green." *Boston Herald* 21 September 2007.

Page 3 *Former Vice President Al Gore* . . . : www.nobelprize.org.

Page 3 *The U.S. government is working* . . . : Fialka, John J., and Kathryn Kranhold. "Lights Out for Old Bulbs?" *The Wall Street Journal* 13 September 2007.

Page 4 *Carbon dioxide is released* . . . : E-mail correspondence with Dr. Susan Hassol, climate analyst and author.

Page 5 *Cars, factories, and electric power plants* . . . : www.fueleconomy.com.

Page 5 *global warming is causing* . . . : Tebaldi, Claudia, et al. "Going to the Extremes: An Intercomparison of Model-Simulated Historical and Future Changes in Extreme Events." *Climatic Change* 79.3/4 (2006): 185–211.

Page 5 *Global warming is also causing less snow* . . . : Stauth, David. "Global Warming Poses Risk to Pacific Northwest Snowpack, Ski Resorts." *Oregon State University News and Communications Services* 7 March 2006.

Page 6 *Both glass-covered greenhouses* . . . : Interview with John Steelman, Campaign Director, Natural Resources Defense Council Climate Center.

Page 8 *The average American adult* . . . : IPCC AR4 WGI, SPM, p. 3.

Page 8 *It's an amount that scientists* . . . : Interview with Tim Greeff, Campaign Director, Natural Resources Defense Council Climate Center.

Page 9 *Using a screensaver* . . . : Correspondence with Noah Horowitz, Senior Scientist, Natural Resources Defense Council; http://www.energystar.gov/index.cfm?c=energy_awareness.bus_energy_use for conversions.

Page 9 *Turning on the lights* . . . : Energy Information Agency, Department of Energy, www.eia.doe.gov.

Page 9 *Taking a bath* . . . : The number is based on a flow rate of 5 gallons per minute into a tub filling in 4 minutes and heating 20 gallons of water, then converting Btu to therms to kWh to pounds of CO_2. Ibid; www.showerheadsrus.com/sp-bin/spirit?page=24&CATALOG=5.

Page 9 *Riding in a car* . . . *(based on driving to school 2.5 miles each way):* The median distance to school for children ages 5–15 years, http://www.cdc.gov/mmwr/preview/mmwrhtml/mm5132al.htm.

Page 9 *. . . in a car that gets 20 miles per gallon:* Conversation with Tim Greeff, Campaign Director, Natural Resources Defense Council Climate Center, for conversions of mpg to lbs of CO_2.

Page 9 *Now, if you take* . . . : U.S. Census Bureau, 2000 Census.

Page 9 *Because CO_2 stays in the atmosphere* . . . : IPCC AR4 WGI, p. 11, "Scientific Assessment of Ozone Depletion," 10.21.

Page 10 *. . . the mayors of 418 cities:* www.sierraclub.org/coolcities.

Page 15 *If every kid in America* . . . : www.energystar.gov.

Page 15 *It would be like* . . . : www.energystar.gov/ia/partners/promotions/change_light/downloads/MayorToolkit.pdf.

Page 17 *Up to 10 percent* . . . : www.eia.doe.gov.

Page 18 *Americans use ten billion* . . . : American Forest and Paper Association. www.reusablebags.com/facts.php.

Page 20 *The more trees* . . . : Natural Resources Defense Council (NRDC). "Fact Sheet: Saving Paper in School."

Page 21 *Bringing in your own* . . . : Environmental Defense Fund.

Page 21 *Last year, one major* . . . : NRDC. *Nature's Voice.*

Page 21 *You want to buy* . . . : NRDC. "Environmentally Preferable Paper: Why and How to Buy It."

Page 21 *Forty percent of the fiber* . . . : Food and Agriculture Orga2ization, FAOSTAT.

Page 21 *Fifteen trees are cut down* . . . : Conservatree. "Trees Into Paper." 2006. www.conservatree.com/learn/EnviroIssues/TreeStats.shtml.

Page 22 *Cars that sit* . . . : U.S. Environmental Protection Agency, Office of Mobile Sources: Fact Sheet OMS-18. "Your Car and Clean Air: What YOU Can Do to Reduce Pollution." August 1994. http://www.epa.gov/otaq/consumer/18-youdo.pdf.

Page 23 *The students of the University of Washington* . . . : Organic Consumers Association. www.organicconsumers.org/2006/article 1797.cfm.

Page 26 *A hybrid is high-tech* . . . : NRDC. "Clean Air and Energy."

Page 27 *When combined with regular gasoline* . . . : "Waste-to-Energy Innovation." *WE Energies.* http://www.we-energies.com/environment/renewable_energy_biomass_tinedale.htm.

Page 28 *The Indy 500* . . . : www.indy500.com/news/story.php?story_id=4105.

Page 28 *An engine running on ethanol* . . . : Jones, Roland. "The Driver's Seat: Ethanol Boosters Hoping for Indy 500 Win." *MSNBC.* 28 May 2006. www.msnbc.msn.com/id/12740848.

Page 29 *Today, a typical wind turbine* . . . : Renewable Energy Systems. www.res-ltd.com/wind-power/faqs.htm.

Page 33 *Recent discoveries* . . . : Woodyard, Chris. "Honda Sees Possible Ethanol Breakthrough—New Microorganism Improves Efficiency." *USA Today* 15 September 2006.

Page 38 *The band Coldplay* . . . : Kher, Unmesh, et al. "How to Seize the Initiative." *Time* 3 April 2006, p. 46.

Page 39 *A company called Simple* . . . : Simple Shoe Company, "a nice little shoe company," www.simpleshoes.com, "Greentoeology," Spring 2007.

Page 39 *Kenny Luna* . . . : E-mail correspondence with Kenny Luna, eighth-grade teacher, at www.thebrightidea.blogspot.com.

Page 39 *Anne Lasker* . . . : Conversation with Anne Lasker, parent and creator of Trashion Show.

Selected Bibliography

Books

Dauncey, Guy, with Patrick Mazza. *Stormy Weather: 101 Solutions to Global Climate Change.* Gabriola Island, British Columbia, Canada: New Society Publishers, 2001.

Flannery, Tim. *The Weather Makers.* New York: Atlantic Monthly Press, 2005.

Gelbspan, Ross. *Boiling Point: How Politicians, Big Oil and Coal, Journalists and Activists Are Fueling the Climate Crisis—and What We Can Do to Avert Disaster.* New York: Basic Books, 2004.

Gore, Al. *An Inconvenient Truth.* New York: Rodale, 2006.

———. *Earth in the Balance: Ecology and the Human Spirit.* Boston: Houghton Mifflin, 2000.

Kolbert, Elizabeth. *Field Notes from a Catastrophe.* New York: Bloomsbury, 2006.

Tennesen, Michael. *The Complete Idiot's Guide to Global Warming.* New York: Alpha Publishing, 2004.

Tickell, Josh. *Biodiesel America: How to Achieve Energy Security, Free America from Middle-East Oil Dependence and Make Money Growing Fuel.* USA: Yorkshire Press, 2006.

Trask, Crissy. *It's Easy Being Green.* Layton, Utah: Gibbs Smith, 2006.

Magazines

BusinessWeek, Global Warming Issue, 16 August 2004.

The Economist, The Heat Is On Issue, September 9–15, 2006.

Mother Jones, As the World Burns Issue, June 2005.

National Geographic, Signs from Earth Issue, September 2004.

Natural History, Cooking the Climate with Coal Issue, May 2006.

Newsweek, Save the Planet — Or Else, 16 April 2007.

onearth, Natural Resources Defense Council magazine, various issues.

Time, Special Report: Global Warming Issue, 3 April 2006.

Time, The Global Warming Survival Guide, 9 April 2007.

Vanity Fair, Green Issue, May 2006.

Vanity Fair, Second Annual Green Issue, May 2007.

Articles and Reports

American Wind Energy Association. "Fact Sheet: Wind Power Today." 2004. www.awea.org.

Augustin, L. "New Evidence Extends Greenhouse Gas Record from Ice Cores by 50 Percent, Adding 210,000 Years." *Science* 25 November 2005.

Australian Academy of Science. "Biomass—the growing energy resource." www.science.org.au/nova/039.

Avant, Bill. "Paper or Plastic? A Simple Question, Right? Wrong!" *The Tennessee Conservationist.* January/February 2006. www.tn.gov/environment/tn_consv/archive/paperplastic.pdf.

Bryant, Dirk, et al. *The Last Frontier Forests: Ecosystems and economies on the edge.* Washington, D.C.: World Resources Institute, 1997.

Carey, John. "Business on a Warmer Planet." *BusinessWeek* 17 July 2006.

CNN: Science and Space, Associated Press. "Study: Earth Hottest in 400 years." 22 June 2006.

Conservatree. "Trees Into Paper." 2006. www.conservatree.com/learn/EnviroIssues/TreeStats.shtml.

Durner, George M., et al. "Predicting the Future Distribution of Polar Bear Habitat in the Polar Basin." U.S. Department of the Interior. U.S. Geological Survey.

Egan, Timothy. "Heat Invades Cool Heights Over Arizona Desert." *The New York Times* 27 March 2007.

Energy Information Administration. *Emissions of Greenhouse Gases in the United States, 2004.* Report #DOE/EIA 0573 (2004), December 2005.

Energy Quest. "Chapter 8: Fossil Fuels." http://www.energyquest.ca.gov/story/chapter08.html.

———. "Chapter 10: Biomass Energy." http://www.energyquest.ca.gov/story/chapter10.html.

———. "Chapter 11: Geothermal Energy." http://www.energyquest.ca.gov/story/chapter11.html.

———. "Chapter 12: Hydro Power." http://www.energyquest.ca.gov/story/chapter12.html.

Fialka, John J., and Kathryn Kranhold. "Lights Out for Old Bulbs?" *The Wall Street Journal* 13 September 2007.

Heinz Center for Science, Economics, and the Environment. *Human Links to Coastal Disasters.* 2002.

Henne, Gudrun, and Christoph Thies. "Will the Last of the Ancient Forests Survive in 2050?" *Unasylva* 52.1 (2001).

"How Do Clouds Form?" *Forecasting the Weather Using Clouds.* 2001. http://snrs.unl.edu/amet351/noehrenberg/cloudformation.html.

Huisman, Jef, et al. Letter. "Reduced Mixing Generates Oscillations and Chaos in the Oceanic Deep Chlorophyll Maximum." *Nature* 439.4074 (2006): 322–325.

Intergovernmental Panel on Climate Change (IPCC). *Third Assessment Report: Climate Change 2001.*

———. *Fourth Assessment Report: Climate Change 2007: Summary for Policy Makers.*

Interstate Renewable Energy Council (IREC). *Schools Going Solar.* www.irecusa.org.

Jones, Roland. "The Driver's Seat: Ethanol Boosters Hoping for Indy 500 Win." *MSNBC.* 28 May 2006. www.msnbc.msn.com/id/12740848.

Kher, Unmesh, et al. "How to Seize the Initiative." *Time* 3 April 2006.

Malcolm, Jay R., et al. "Global Warming and Extinctions of Endemic Species from Biodiversity Hotspots." *Conservation Biology* 20.2 (2006): 538–548.

Marshall, Gareth, et al. "The Impact of a Changing Southern Hemisphere Annular Mode on Antarctic Peninsula Summer Temperatures." *Journal of Climate* 19.20 (2006): 5388–5404.

McFarling, Usha Lee. "Altered Oceans: A Chemical Imbalance." *Los Angeles Times* 3 August 2006.

McGahee, Alvin L. National Oceanic Atmospheric Administration: National Climate Data Center (NCDC), United States Department of Commerce. *Selected U.S. City and State Extremes for July 2006.*

Mohan, Jacqueline E., et al. "Biomass and Toxicity Responses of Poison Ivy to Elevated Atmospheric CO_2." *PNAS* 103.24 (2006): 9086–9089.

"NASA Survey Confirms Climate Warming Impact on Polar Ice Sheets: Release 06–089." National Aeronautic and Space Administration. 8 March 2006. http://www.nasa.gov/home/hqnews/2006/mar/HQ_06089_polar_ice_sheets_melting.html.

"National Assessment of Coastal Vulnerability to Future Sea Level Rise: Report Number 076-00." *U.S. Geological Survey.* June 2000. http://pubs.usgs.gov/fs/fs76-00/fs076-00.pdf.

Natural Resources Defense Council. "Hybrid Values." www.nrdc.org/air/transportation/ghybrid.asp.

———. "Environmentally Preferable Paper: Why and How to Buy It." *Paper Industry Reform Project,* January 2005.

———. "Fact Sheet: Saving Paper in School." www.nrdc.org/greensquad/library/paper.html.

———. *Nature's Voice*. January/February 2005.

"Ocean Acidification Due to Increasing Atmospheric Carbon Dioxide." *The Royal Society*. 30 June 2005.

Patz, Jonathan, et al. "Impact of Regional Climate Change on Human Health." *Nature* 438.7066 (2005): 310–317.

Poggioli, Sylvia. "Climate Change Threatens European Landmarks." *NPR Morning Edition* 17 August 2007.

Ruttimann, Jacqueline. "Oceanography: Sick Seas." *Nature* 442.7106 (2006): 978–980.

Santer, B. D., et al. "Forced and Unforced Ocean Temperature Changes in Atlantic and Pacific Tropical Cyclogenesis Regions. *PNAS* 103.38 (2006): 13905–13910.

Siegenthaler, Urs, et al. "Stable Carbon Cycle-Climate Relationship During the Late Pleistocene." *Science* 310 (2005): 1313–1317.

Stauth, David. "Global Warming Poses Risk to Pacific Northwest Snowpack, Ski Resorts." *Oregon State University News and Communications Services* 7 March 2006.

"Students recognized for outstanding energy projects." National Energy Education Development Project. 1 May 2007. http://www.need.org/needpdf/07pressindschool.pdf.

Tebaldi, Claudia, et al. "Going to the Extremes: An Intercomparison of Model-Simulated Historical and Future Changes in Extreme Events." *Climatic Change* 79.3/4 (2006): 185–211.

Texas A&M Student Counseling Services. "Top Jobs in Energy-Related Industries." www.scs.tamu.edu/articles/hotocs0805.asp.

Thomas, Chris D., et al. "Extinction Risk from Climate Change." *Nature* 427.6970 (2004): 145–147.

U.S. Environmental Protection Agency. "Drinking Water." www.epa.gov/region7/kids/drnk_b.htm.

———. "Recycling." http://www.epa.gov/epaoswer/non-hw/muncpl/recycle.htm.

———. "Conservation." www.epa.gov.

———. Office of Mobile Sources: Fact Sheet OMS-18. "Your Car and Clean Air: What YOU Can Do to Reduce Pollution." August 1994. http://www.epa.gov/otaq/consumer/18-youdo.pdf.

Van Voorhis, Scott. "Wally Would Be Proud as Fenway Park Goes Green." *Boston Herald* 21 September 2007.

"Waste-to-Energy Innovation." *WE Energies*. http://www.we-energies.com/environment/renewable_energy_biomass_tinedale.htm.

Woodyard, Chris. "Honda Sees Possible Ethanol Breakthrough—New Microorganism Improves Efficiency." *USA Today* 15 September 2006.

Zwally, H. Jay, and Konrad Steffan. "Surface Melt-Induced Acceleration of Greenland Ice-Sheet Flow." *Science Express* 297 (2002): 218–212.

Web Sites

American Forest and Paper Association. www.afandpaorg.

Energy Star. www.energystar.gov/ia/partners/promotions/change_light/downloads/MayorToolkit.pdf.

Environmental Defense Fund. www.environmentaldefense.org.

Food and Agricultural Organization of the United Nations, FAOSTAT. www.faostat.fao.org.

Green dream jobs. www.sustainablebusiness.com/jobs.

Indianapolis 500. www.indy500.com/news/story.php?story_id=4105.

National Climatic Data Center (NCDC). www.ncdc.noaa.gov.

National Resources Defense Council (NRDC). www.nrdc.org.

The Nature Conservancy. www.nature.org.

The Nobel Prize. www.nobelprize.org.

Renewable Energy Access. www.renewableenergyaccess.com/rea/jobs/home.

Sierra Club. www.sierraclub.org.

U.S. Census Bureau, 2000. www.census.gov/population/www/socdemo/age.html.

U.S. Department of Energy. Energy Efficiency and Renewable Energy. www.fueleconomy.com.

———. Energy Efficiency and Renewable Energy, Alternative Fuels Data Center. www.eere.energy.gov.

———. Energy Information Agency. www.eia.doe.gov.

Renewable Energy Systems. www.res-ltd.com/wind-power/faqs.htm.

World Wildlife Fund. www.worldwildlife.org.

Interviews and Correspondence

Eric Chivian M.D., Director, Center for Health and the Global Environment, Harvard Medical School.

Dr. Heidi Cullen, The Weather Channel climate expert and host of *The Climate Code*.

Richard Fox, Surveys Manager, Butterfly Conservation Initiative.

Tim Greeff, Campaign Director, Natural Resources Defense Council Climate Center.

Dr. Susan Hassol, climate analyst and author.

Noah Horowitz, Senior Scientist, Natural Resources Defense Council.

Daniel A. Lashof, Ph.D., Science Director, Natural Resources Defense Council Climate Center.

Anne Lasker, parent and creator of Trashion Show.

Kenny Luna, eighth-grade teacher.

Dr. Gareth Marshall, climatologist, British Antarctic Survey.

Nigel Pervis, The Nature Conservancy.

Joel Reynolds, Director, Natural Resources Defense Council Marine Mammal Protection Program.

John Steelman, Campaign Director, Natural Resources Defense Council Climate Center.

Eric Wolff, British Antarctic Survey.

Photo Credits

Grateful acknowledgment is made for permission to reprint the following:

All illustrations by Stephen Schudlich.

Page i, globe: NASA. *Pages 4–5, grass:* © jallfree/iStockphoto.com, 1933744; *globe:* NASA; blanketed chair: © Johan Odmann/Johner Images/ Getty Images, 72163467; *pizza:* © Vasko Miokovic/iStockphoto, 1933040. *Page 6, Whoopie Cushion:* © PunchStock, TOY04983-00; *cow:* © Joy Brown/Shutterstock Inc., 1881097. *Page 7, Popsicle:* © Kate Tero/iStockphoto 2004834. *Page 8, footprint:* © James Levin, DSC_3661. *Pages 10–11, U.S. Capitol Building:* © Randy Wells/Stone/Getty Images, 454610-001. *Page 12, Portland bike lane:* © Jonathan Maus/BikePortland.org, DSC_1910. *Page 14, compact fluorescent lightbulb:* © Albert Lozano/Shutterstock Inc., 1041557; *girl:* © Steve Craft/Iconica/Getty Images, 200348188-002. *Page 16, wall with outlet:* © Creasence/Shutterstock Inc., 2915616; *Energy Star logo:* Courtesy Energy Star, U.S. Environmental Protection Agency. *Page 17, plugs with cords:* Anthony Berenyi/Shutterstock Inc., 2616366. *Page 18, paper bag:* © Photos.com, 8020375; *plastic bag:* © Stephen Stickler/Photographer's Choice/Getty Images, 200470838-001; *canvas bag:* © James Levin, DSC_4013. *Page 20, Muir Woods:* Walter Meayers Edwards/National Geographic/Getty Images, ngs0_8548. *Pages 22–23, sky:* © Corbis Photography (RF)/Veer, CBP1001034; *notepaper:* © Siede Preis/Photodisc (RF)/Getty Images, AA003104. *Page 24, sky:* © Corbis Photography (RF)/Veer, CBP1001034; *notepaper:* © Siede Preis/Photodisc (RF)/Getty Images, AA003104; *classroom:* © Stockbyte Photography (RF)/Veer, SBP0353011. *Page 25, school with solar panels:* Courtesy Glen Kizer for Foundation for Environmental Education. *Page 26, NYC city bus:* Courtesy Ernie Mauro, BAE Systems; *Prius:* Courtesy, © 2007 Toyota Motor Sales, U.S.A., INC. *Page 27, wheat field:* © Harald Sund/Photographer's Choice/Getty Images, 200364465-001; *flex-fuel car:* Josiah Cuneo/ Courtesy greasecar.com. *Page 28, Indy 500:* Courtesy Indy Racing League, indycar.com, photographer Chris Jones. *Page 29, wind turbine farm:* © Rafa Irusta/ Shutterstock Inc., 1242320. *Page 30, Dell-Winston solar car:* Courtesy Dell-Winston School Solar Car Challenge. *Page 31, Old Faithful:* © Emanuele Taroni/ Photodisc (RF)/ Getty Images, AA019665. *Page 32, Grand Coulee Dam:* © Philip Gendreau/Bettmann/Corbis, GNGN388. *Page 33, wood chips:* © Elena Elisseeva/ Shutterstock Inc., 3039011. *Pages 34–35, sky:* © Corbis Photography (RF)/Veer, CBP1001034. *Page 36, sky:* © Corbis Photography (RF)/Veer, CBP1001034; *Gro Harlem Brundtland:* © Ralph Orlowski/Getty Images, 52193186. *Page 37, Eagles logo:* Courtesy Philadelphia Eagles; *Paul Frank logo:* Courtesy Paul Frank; *Ugg logo:* Courtesy Ugg Austrailia; *MTV logo:* Courtesy thinkmtv. *Page 38, Coldplay:* © Kevin Westenberg/Courtesy 3 D Management. *Page 39, globe:* NASA. *Page 40, Stopglobalwarming.org logo:* Courtesy Laurie David and The Tide Center. *Page 45, sky:* © Corbis Photography (RF)/Veer, CBP1001034; *authors:* Stacie Isabella Turk, Ribbonhead. *Page 46, Stopglobalwarming.org logo:* Courtesy Laurie David and The Tide Center.

About the Authors

Laurie David is a global warming activist and the producer of the Academy Award-winning film *An Inconvenient Truth* and the HBO documentary *Too Hot Not to Handle*. She executive-produced *Earth to America!*, a primetime comedy special about global warming, which earned her a Gracie Allen Award for Individual Achievement. A trustee of the Natural Resources Defense Council, Laurie founded the Stop Global Warming Virtual March with Senator John McCain and Robert F. Kennedy, Jr. She was the first-ever guest editor of the green May 2006 and 2007 issues of *Elle* magazine. In 2006 Laurie published her first book, the bestseller *Stop Global Warming: The Solution Is You*. She also launched the Stop Global Warming College Tour with Sheryl Crow, on which they visited college campuses throughout the Southeast on a biodiesel tour bus.

Laurie David received the prestigious Stanley Kramer Award from the Producers Guild of America and a Humanitas Prize Special Award for *An Inconvenient Truth*. She has been honored with the Audubon Society's Rachel Carson Award, the Feminist Majority's Eleanor Roosevelt Award, the NRDC's 2006 Forces for Nature Award, and by Robert F. Kennedy Jr.'s Riverkeeper organization.

Laurie, a regular blogger on the Huffington Post, has been featured on such shows as *Oprah*, *Good Morning America*, and on CNN and has been profiled in numerous magazines, including *Vanity Fair*, which called her the "Bono of climate change." She lives in Los Angeles, California.

Cambria Gordon is an award-winning former advertising copywriter who now pursues children's writing full-time. Her credits include a nonfiction book, *Fifty Nifty Crafts to Make With Things Around the House*, and an episode for the award-winning animated Disney Channel series *Madeline*.

Cambria is an active environmentalist and lives with her husband and their three children in Los Angeles, California.

stopglobalwarming.org